This Client Book Belongs To:

Name: ______________________

Company: ______________________

Address: ______________________

____

License: ______________________

Log Number: ______________________

Dates: __________ to __________

Phone: ______________________

Fax: ______________________

eMail: ______________________

Website: ______________________

Facebook: ______________________

Instagram: ______________________

Twitter: ______________________

Other: ______________________

____

____

Index

Client / Customer	Page

Index

Client / Customer	Page

Index

Client / Customer	Page

Index

Client / Customer	Page

Index

Client / Customer	Page

Client Information

Name:	
Address:	
Phone:	
eMail:	
Notes:	

Date	Time	Service / Work	Price	Notes

Client Information

Name:	
Address:	
Phone:	
eMail:	
Notes:	

Date	Time	Service / Work	Price	Notes

Client Information

Name:	
Address:	
Phone:	
eMail:	
Notes:	

Date	Time	Service / Work	Price	Notes

Client Information

Name:	
Address:	
Phone:	
eMail:	
Notes:	

Date	Time	Service / Work	Price	Notes

Client Information

Name:	
Address:	
Phone:	
eMail:	
Notes:	

Date	Time	Service / Work	Price	Notes

Client Information

Name:	
Address:	
Phone:	
eMail:	
Notes:	

Date	Time	Service / Work	Price	Notes

Client Information

Name:	
Address:	
Phone:	
eMail:	
Notes:	

Date	Time	Service / Work	Price	Notes

Client Information

Name:	
Address:	
Phone:	
eMail:	
Notes:	

Date	Time	Service / Work	Price	Notes

Client Information

Name:	
Address:	
Phone:	
eMail:	
Notes:	

Date	Time	Service / Work	Price	Notes

Client Information

Name:	
Address:	
Phone:	
eMail:	
Notes:	

Date	Time	Service / Work	Price	Notes

Client Information

Name:	
Address:	
Phone:	
eMail:	
Notes:	

Date	Time	Service / Work	Price	Notes

Client Information

Name:	
Address:	
Phone:	
eMail:	
Notes:	

Date	Time	Service / Work	Price	Notes

Client Information

Name:	
Address:	
Phone:	
eMail:	
Notes:	

Date	Time	Service / Work	Price	Notes

Client Information

Name:	
Address:	
Phone:	
eMail:	
Notes:	

Date	Time	Service / Work	Price	Notes

Client Information

Name:	
Address:	
Phone:	
eMail:	
Notes:	

Date	Time	Service / Work	Price	Notes

Client Information

Name:	
Address:	
Phone:	
eMail:	
Notes:	

Date	Time	Service / Work	Price	Notes

Client Information

Name:	
Address:	
Phone:	
eMail:	
Notes:	

Date	Time	Service / Work	Price	Notes

Client Information

Name:	
Address:	
Phone:	
eMail:	
Notes:	

Date	Time	Service / Work	Price	Notes

Client Information

Name:	
Address:	
Phone:	
eMail:	
Notes:	

Date	Time	Service / Work	Price	Notes

Client Information

Name:	
Address:	
Phone:	
eMail:	
Notes:	

Date	Time	Service / Work	Price	Notes

Client Information

Name:	
Address:	
Phone:	
eMail:	
Notes:	

Date	Time	Service / Work	Price	Notes

Client Information

Name:	
Address:	
Phone:	
eMail:	
Notes:	

Date	Time	Service / Work	Price	Notes

Client Information

Name:	
Address:	
Phone:	
eMail:	
Notes:	

Date	Time	Service / Work	Price	Notes

Client Information

Name:	
Address:	
Phone:	
eMail:	
Notes:	

Date	Time	Service / Work	Price	Notes

Client Information

Name:	
Address:	
Phone:	
eMail:	
Notes:	

Date	Time	Service / Work	Price	Notes

Client Information

Name:	
Address:	
Phone:	
eMail:	
Notes:	

Date	Time	Service / Work	Price	Notes

Client Information

Name:	
Address:	
Phone:	
eMail:	
Notes:	

Date	Time	Service / Work	Price	Notes

Client Information

Name:	
Address:	
Phone:	
eMail:	
Notes:	

Date	Time	Service / Work	Price	Notes

Client Information

Name:	
Address:	
Phone:	
eMail:	
Notes:	

Date	Time	Service / Work	Price	Notes

Client Information

Name:	
Address:	
Phone:	
eMail:	
Notes:	

Date	Time	Service / Work	Price	Notes

Client Information

Name:	
Address:	
Phone:	
eMail:	
Notes:	

Date	Time	Service / Work	Price	Notes

Client Information

Name:	
Address:	
Phone:	
eMail:	
Notes:	

Date	Time	Service / Work	Price	Notes

Client Information

Name:	
Address:	
Phone:	
eMail:	
Notes:	

Date	Time	Service / Work	Price	Notes

Client Information

Name:	
Address:	
Phone:	
eMail:	
Notes:	

Date	Time	Service / Work	Price	Notes

Client Information

Name:	
Address:	
Phone:	
eMail:	
Notes:	

Date	Time	Service / Work	Price	Notes

Client Information

Name:	
Address:	
Phone:	
eMail:	
Notes:	

Date	Time	Service / Work	Price	Notes

Client Information

Name:	
Address:	
Phone:	
eMail:	
Notes:	

Date	Time	Service / Work	Price	Notes

Client Information

Name:	
Address:	
Phone:	
eMail:	
Notes:	

Date	Time	Service / Work	Price	Notes

Client Information

Name:	
Address:	
Phone:	
eMail:	
Notes:	

Date	Time	Service / Work	Price	Notes

Client Information

Name:	
Address:	
Phone:	
eMail:	
Notes:	

Date	Time	Service / Work	Price	Notes

Client Information

Name:	
Address:	
Phone:	
eMail:	
Notes:	

Date	Time	Service / Work	Price	Notes

Client Information

Name:	
Address:	
Phone:	
eMail:	
Notes:	

Date	Time	Service / Work	Price	Notes

Client Information

Name:	
Address:	
Phone:	
eMail:	
Notes:	

Date	Time	Service / Work	Price	Notes

Client Information

Name:	
Address:	
Phone:	
eMail:	
Notes:	

Date	Time	Service / Work	Price	Notes

Client Information

Name:	
Address:	
Phone:	
eMail:	
Notes:	

Date	Time	Service / Work	Price	Notes

Client Information

Name:	
Address:	
Phone:	
eMail:	
Notes:	

Date	Time	Service / Work	Price	Notes

Client Information

Name:	
Address:	
Phone:	
eMail:	
Notes:	

Date	Time	Service / Work	Price	Notes

Client Information

Name:	
Address:	
Phone:	
eMail:	
Notes:	

Date	Time	Service / Work	Price	Notes

Client Information

Name:	
Address:	
Phone:	
eMail:	
Notes:	

Date	Time	Service / Work	Price	Notes

Client Information

Name:	
Address:	
Phone:	
eMail:	
Notes:	

Date	Time	Service / Work	Price	Notes

Client Information

Name:	
Address:	
Phone:	
eMail:	
Notes:	

Date	Time	Service / Work	Price	Notes

Client Information

Name:	
Address:	
Phone:	
eMail:	
Notes:	

Date	Time	Service / Work	Price	Notes

Client Information

Name:	
Address:	
Phone:	
eMail:	
Notes:	

Date	Time	Service / Work	Price	Notes

Client Information

Name:	
Address:	
Phone:	
eMail:	
Notes:	

Date	Time	Service / Work	Price	Notes

Client Information

Name:	
Address:	
Phone:	
eMail:	
Notes:	

Date	Time	Service / Work	Price	Notes

Client Information

Name:	
Address:	
Phone:	
eMail:	
Notes:	

Date	Time	Service / Work	Price	Notes

Client Information

Name:	
Address:	
Phone:	
eMail:	
Notes:	

Date	Time	Service / Work	Price	Notes

Client Information

Name:	
Address:	
Phone:	
eMail:	
Notes:	

Date	Time	Service / Work	Price	Notes

Client Information

Name:	
Address:	
Phone:	
eMail:	
Notes:	

Date	Time	Service / Work	Price	Notes

Client Information

Name:	
Address:	
Phone:	
eMail:	
Notes:	

Date	Time	Service / Work	Price	Notes

Client Information

Name:	
Address:	
Phone:	
eMail:	
Notes:	

Date	Time	Service / Work	Price	Notes

Client Information

Name:	
Address:	
Phone:	
eMail:	
Notes:	

Date	Time	Service / Work	Price	Notes

Client Information

Name:	
Address:	
Phone:	
eMail:	
Notes:	

Date	Time	Service / Work	Price	Notes

Client Information

Name:	
Address:	
Phone:	
eMail:	
Notes:	

Date	Time	Service / Work	Price	Notes

Client Information

Name:	
Address:	
Phone:	
eMail:	
Notes:	

Date	Time	Service / Work	Price	Notes

Client Information

Name:	
Address:	
Phone:	
eMail:	
Notes:	

Date	Time	Service / Work	Price	Notes

Client Information

Name:	
Address:	
Phone:	
eMail:	
Notes:	

Date	Time	Service / Work	Price	Notes

Client Information

Name:	
Address:	
Phone:	
eMail:	
Notes:	

Date	Time	Service / Work	Price	Notes

Client Information

Name:	
Address:	
Phone:	
eMail:	
Notes:	

Date	Time	Service / Work	Price	Notes

Client Information

Name:	
Address:	
Phone:	
eMail:	
Notes:	

Date	Time	Service / Work	Price	Notes

Client Information

Name:	
Address:	
Phone:	
eMail:	
Notes:	

Date	Time	Service / Work	Price	Notes

Client Information

Name:	
Address:	
Phone:	
eMail:	
Notes:	

Date	Time	Service / Work	Price	Notes

Client Information

Name:	
Address:	
Phone:	
eMail:	
Notes:	

Date	Time	Service / Work	Price	Notes

Client Information

Name:	
Address:	
Phone:	
eMail:	
Notes:	

Date	Time	Service / Work	Price	Notes

Client Information

Name:	
Address:	
Phone:	
eMail:	
Notes:	

Date	Time	Service / Work	Price	Notes

Client Information

Name:	
Address:	
Phone:	
eMail:	
Notes:	

Date	Time	Service / Work	Price	Notes

Client Information

Name:	
Address:	
Phone:	
eMail:	
Notes:	

Date	Time	Service / Work	Price	Notes

Client Information

Name:	
Address:	
Phone:	
eMail:	
Notes:	

Date	Time	Service / Work	Price	Notes

Client Information

Name:	
Address:	
Phone:	
eMail:	
Notes:	

Date	Time	Service / Work	Price	Notes

Client Information

Name:	
Address:	
Phone:	
eMail:	
Notes:	

Date	Time	Service / Work	Price	Notes

Client Information

Name:	
Address:	
Phone:	
eMail:	
Notes:	

Date	Time	Service / Work	Price	Notes

Client Information

Name:	
Address:	
Phone:	
eMail:	
Notes:	

Date	Time	Service / Work	Price	Notes

Client Information

Name:	
Address:	
Phone:	
eMail:	
Notes:	

Date	Time	Service / Work	Price	Notes

Client Information

Name:	
Address:	
Phone:	
eMail:	
Notes:	

Date	Time	Service / Work	Price	Notes

Client Information

Name:	
Address:	
Phone:	
eMail:	
Notes:	

Date	Time	Service / Work	Price	Notes

Client Information

Name:	
Address:	
Phone:	
eMail:	
Notes:	

Date	Time	Service / Work	Price	Notes

Client Information

Name:	
Address:	
Phone:	
eMail:	
Notes:	

Date	Time	Service / Work	Price	Notes

Client Information

Name:	
Address:	
Phone:	
eMail:	
Notes:	

Date	Time	Service / Work	Price	Notes

Client Information

Name:	
Address:	
Phone:	
eMail:	
Notes:	

Date	Time	Service / Work	Price	Notes

Client Information

Name:	
Address:	
Phone:	
eMail:	
Notes:	

Date	Time	Service / Work	Price	Notes

Client Information

Name:	
Address:	
Phone:	
eMail:	
Notes:	

Date	Time	Service / Work	Price	Notes

Client Information

Name:	
Address:	
Phone:	
eMail:	
Notes:	

Date	Time	Service / Work	Price	Notes

Client Information

Name:	
Address:	
Phone:	
eMail:	
Notes:	

Date	Time	Service / Work	Price	Notes

Client Information

Name:	
Address:	
Phone:	
eMail:	
Notes:	

Date	Time	Service / Work	Price	Notes

Client Information

Name:	
Address:	
Phone:	
eMail:	
Notes:	

Date	Time	Service / Work	Price	Notes

Client Information

Name:	
Address:	
Phone:	
eMail:	
Notes:	

Date	Time	Service / Work	Price	Notes

Client Information

Name:	
Address:	
Phone:	
eMail:	
Notes:	

Date	Time	Service / Work	Price	Notes

Client Information

Name:	
Address:	
Phone:	
eMail:	
Notes:	

Date	Time	Service / Work	Price	Notes

Client Information

Name:	
Address:	
Phone:	
eMail:	
Notes:	

Date	Time	Service / Work	Price	Notes

Client Information

Name:	
Address:	
Phone:	
eMail:	
Notes:	

Date	Time	Service / Work	Price	Notes

Client Information

Name:	
Address:	
Phone:	
eMail:	
Notes:	

Date	Time	Service / Work	Price	Notes

Client Information

Name:	
Address:	
Phone:	
eMail:	
Notes:	

Date	Time	Service / Work	Price	Notes

Made in United States
Orlando, FL
18 June 2025

62191174R00063